BEI GRIN MACHT SICH IHR
WISSEN BEZAHLT

- Wir veröffentlichen Ihre Hausarbeit,
  Bachelor- und Masterarbeit

- Ihr eigenes eBook und Buch -
  weltweit in allen wichtigen Shops

- Verdienen Sie an jedem Verkauf

Jetzt bei www.GRIN.com hochladen
und kostenlos publizieren

Deborah De Lorenzo

The psychological aspect of aging in Edward Albee's "Three Tall Women"

GRIN Verlag

Bibliografische Information der Deutschen Nationalbibliothek:

Die Deutsche Bibliothek verzeichnet diese Publikation in der Deutschen National-
bibliografie; detaillierte bibliografische Daten sind im Internet über http://dnb.d-
nb.de/ abrufbar.

Impressum:

Copyright © 2013 GRIN Verlag GmbH
Druck und Bindung: Books on Demand GmbH, Norderstedt Germany
ISBN: 978-3-656-59441-3

Dieses Buch bei GRIN:

http://www.grin.com/de/e-book/268025/the-psychological-aspect-of-aging-in-
edward-albee-s-three-tall-women

GRIN - Your knowledge has value

Der GRIN Verlag publiziert seit 1998 wissenschaftliche Arbeiten von Studenten, Hochschullehrern und anderen Akademikern als eBook und gedrucktes Buch. Die Verlagswebsite www.grin.com ist die ideale Plattform zur Veröffentlichung von Hausarbeiten, Abschlussarbeiten, wissenschaftlichen Aufsätzen, Dissertationen und Fachbüchern.

Besuchen Sie uns im Internet:

http://www.grin.com/

http://www.facebook.com/grincom

http://www.twitter.com/grin_com

Oberstufe
Schultheißallee 1
90478 Nürnberg
Tel. (0911) 47 49 19 27 / 47 49 19-0
www.martin-behaim-gymnasium.de

Martin-
Behaim-
Gymnasium
Nürnberg

Naturwissenschaftlich-
technologisches und
Sprachliches Gymnasium

Oberstufenjahrgang 2012/2014
Seminararbeit

Thema: The psychological aspect of aging in Edward Albee's <u>Three Tall Women</u>

Rahmenthema: The American Drama of the 20th Century

Verfasser: Deborah De Lorenzo

Wissenschaftspropädeutisches Seminar: 1W1,
The American Drama of the 20th Century

Abgabetermin: 12.11.2013

Erzielte Punkte: .... **in Worten:** ....

....
Unterschrift des Seminarleiters

Table of contents

1. Introduction: How does one become the person one is?

In the course of a human's life a person goes through different physical and psychological stages and as the body becomes older the mind follows and vice versa. Already Greek and Roman philosophy discussed negative and positive aspects of different stages of human life. The first theoretical disquisitions on human psychological development were composed as early as in the 18th century. During this time Johannes Nikolaus Tetens described human development as a lifelong process including gain and loss and affected by sociocultural aspects; a process that therefore can be influenced. The Belgian mathematician Adolphe Quételet dealt with the development of skills and collected empirical data on the course of human life. He did not base his work only on statistics about physical aspects, such as height, weight and strength but also and more importantly on psychological variables, like emotions and intellectual potential. He also covered how historical events influenced aging, hence how the psyche and emotional condition of a person influence how old people become (see Lang/Martin/Pinquart: Entwicklungspsychologie – Erwachsenenalter, p.14). It is apparent that the interest in the human psyche and its effect on aging as a process were always of scientific concern. It is something we face daily.

Edward Albee's Three Tall Women perfectly represents the issue of developmental psychology. One protagonist is being portrayed by three versions of herself at different stages of her life and as a result the development of that protagonist becomes clear. An array of changes in her behavior and in her way of thinking can be seen. The most important point of the protagonist's unfolding, just as Johannes Nikolaus Tetens describes, lies in the influence of one´s social surroundings (see Lang/Martin/Pinquart: Entwicklungspsychologie – Erwachsenenalter, p.14).

The topic "The psychological aspect of aging in Edward Albee's Three Tall Women" focuses on the protagonist's social development as she gets older. In this paper the character of the protagonist will be analyzed and the courses of events in her life which lead her to become the person she turns out to be in the end. Following that the most essential themes of the play will be analyzed on the background of psychological aspects. But at first there will be a brief section of information on the playwright and the play itself.

4

2. Edward Albee's play Three Tall Women

The origin of Three Tall Women is the Austrian Vienna's English Theatre, where Franz Schafranek had produced the play for the first time in 1991 and Edward Albee as the author took over the role of the director. After its debut Albee was given the Pulitzer Prize and was nominated for the Drama Desk Award Outstanding Play for Three Tall Women three years later. The play was originally written in English, however Alissa Walser and Martin Walser translated the play into German.

2.1. The playwright Edward Albee

Edward Franklin Albee was born in Virginia in the US in 1928. As a baby he was adopted by the Albees of Larchmont in New York. His family's "wealth and social position [came; DD] from the family's interest in a national chain of theaters".[1] His love for writing was kindled at the age of 20. As an author he wrote several memorable books and plays. His well-known opus "Who's Afraid of Virginia Woolf?" was later filmed and directed by himself. In the United States his work was recognized with several awards. He also received acknowledgement for his writing in German-speaking countries. His first piece of work "The Zoo Story" had its debut performance in Berlin and he was renowned for his work in Austria as well.[2] Edward Albee had no offspring. His sexual orientation was formed when he was "twelve and a half"[3] as he admitted himself. He handles his sexuality in a very neutral way: "I am not a gay writer. I am a writer who happens to be gay."[4] For more than 20 years he shared his existence with Jonathan Thomas, who died in 2005.[5]

2.2. The play in context

It is certain that Three Tall Women is written as an autobiographical piece (see Zinman, 2008, p.118 f.). In the play we face a woman dealing with her homosexual son in an intolerant way. Their relationship fails when the protagonist throws her son out from home because of his sexuality. The same happened to Albee when he turned eighteen. His adoptive mother, Francis Cotter Albee, did not want to allow him to stay at home for the reason that he was gay. This makes it clear that Edward Albee and his adoptive

---

[1] http://www.achievement.org/autodoc/page/alb1bio-1, 20.05.2013.
[2] http://www.achievement.org/autodoc/page/alb1int-1, 25.05.2013.
[3] http://www.npr.org/2011/06/06/136923478/playwright-edward-albee-defends-remarks, 25.05.2013.
[4] ibid.
[5] ibid.

mother had a difficult relationship. "We [he and his mother; DD] had managed to make each other very unhappy over the years, [...] it is true I don't like her much"[6] is what he concedes. This clearly shows that Albee's mother bothered him. He thought of her in contrasting ways. On the one hand he could not stand her intolerance towards his homosexuality; on the other hand he admires her because of her pride and self-assurance (see Zinman, 2008, Albee, p.119). By writing Three Tall Women he comes to terms with that issue in his life. The fact that the drama was written soon after the death of Edward Albee's adoptive mother supports the statement that Three Tall Women is an autobiographical play.[7]

2.3. Content of the play

In the whole drama only three women are introduced as talking characters. The main focus lies on A, who owns the flat where the drama takes place. She is a 92-year-old woman. In the first act the audience gets to know stories of A's life, because she tells her caretaker B about them. C, who visits A as part of her job - she is a young lawyer - which consists of taking care of A's funds. When she comes to the point where she talks about her most aching memories she suddenly discontinues. After B and C realized that she has had a stroke they want to contact A's doctor and her only son.

In the second act of the play all of the three ladies appear again. Therein Edward Albee uses the coup de théâtre (see Zinman, 2008, p.119). Following that dramatic application the three tall women turn out to be one person in different stages of her life. Because of A's look-alike doll that is laying in bed motionless it can be assumed that the protagonist is recalling her life with visions of herself at the ages of 26 and 52. Thereby she is conducting her last conversation with herself in order to be able to rest in peace. Toby Zinman describes that as a "human interior drama".[8]

3. Analysis of the play with respect to the psychological aspect of aging

Since the play is written autobiographically it is said that "the play never feels vicious or vengeful, just as it does not feel maudlin or nostalgic. Psychologically, then, the play would seem to be an extraordinary achievement."[9] Although the literature is

---

[6] Zinman: Edward Albee (2008), p.119.

[7] http://www.courttheatre.org/season/show/three_tall_women/, 21.05.2013.

[8] Zinman: Edward Albee (2008), p.120.

[9] ibid.: p. 119.

6

autobiographical and the psychological aspect does not play the biggest role it is interesting to open one´s mind and take a look behind the scenes to understand the characters' behavior and its background. Not by analyzing the protagonists as Edward Albee´s mother but instead by analyzing the woman that appears in <u>Three Tall Women</u>.

3.1. Analysis of the protagonist and her life

The play is written as a dialogue between only A, B and C, all representing the same woman but at different times of her life. In the first act A, B and C are introduced as three different people with no close relation to each other. In this manner the audience gets acquainted with each of the women as their own character (see Zinman, 2008, p.119). Nevertheless, several allusions are made throughout the first act that show A, B and C are actually one woman, as for example when B tells C with a *"(Sour smile.)* Well ... you just *wait."*[10] as well as when A talks about C: "Oh, she´ll learn"[11] and repeats that on the following page. From the interaction between the three women in act one the audience can deduct their characters and social behavior.

3.1.1. The characters A, B and C

The audience gets to know C as "the emissary from A´s lawyer´s office".[12] She appears to be confident, naive, egocentric and a bit cocky because of her youth as for instance when she says to A implying that she is wrong about her age: *"(A bit as if to a child.)* Well, one of you might be wrong, and it might not be him [, her son; DD]."[13] Her behavior towards A can be generally described as rude and inappropriate as she mocks her and laughs about A (see Albee, 1994, p.12 ff.). She reveals that she does not have much experience with old people by asking B in an aside: "Is it always like this?"[14] Towards the end of the first act she actually admits: "I'm not good at ... all that [dealing with old people; DD]."[15] At this point B mentions for the last time the fact that they are actually one person by telling C: "You'll get there." and "[...]: if you live long enough you won't have to; you'll be

---

[10] Albee: <u>Three Tall Women</u> (1994), p.11.
[11] ibid.: p.13.
[12] Zinman: Edward Albee (2008), p. 120.
[13] Albee: <u>Three Tall Women</u> (1994), p.6.
[14] ibid.: p.12.
[15] ibid.: p.30.

there."[16], which becomes obvious in the second act when she is revealed to be the 26-year-old version of A. Then her attitude remains the same and she "continues to be shallow and irritating"[17]. The explanation for the missing depth in C's character can be explained by the fact that Albee didn't know his mother when she was young and C "thus [is; DD] a mere assumption"[18] on his part. It is a very probable assumption though as in the psychological theories by Costa and McCrae it is said that younger people are more extroverted and open to new experiences in comparison with older ones (see Lang/Martin/Pinquart, 2012, p.150- 151).

B has different attributes in front of the audience. On the one hand she is the care-taker of A and rebukes C by saying "Shhhhhhh"[19] when she is being inappropriate. At the same time she is just doing her job and actually behaves indifferent towards A´s stories. "So you say" [20] is one of her reactions, when A tells them that she loved horse riding. Partly she corrects A, for example when A states that she manages her own business by answering "And *I'll* watch you *pretend* to handle [your affairs; DD]." [21] B also uses sarcasm as an illustration when A says to B that she wants her to tumble:" Yes, I want you to fall;[…] and shatter in … ten pieces." [22] But the major part of her behavior is to be found in her outlook of life. B is the middle-aged one and thus stands in the midpoint of her life. She looks back and remembers an unacceptable past on her part (see Albee, 1994, p.34). That is what makes her the most embittered character in that circle. She thinks a lot of death and sees no real sense in life and lets the people around her know (see Albee, 1994, p.9 f.). This is explainable with the theory by Erik Erikson, who says that middle-aged people struggle with intimacy and stagnate (see Lang/Martin/Pinquart, 2012, p.32). In the case of B, who represents the 52-year-old version of A, you get to know that she cannot cope with her husband´s infidelity as she says: "(*Remembering.*) Who´s he [, her husband; DD] doing it with?[…] who he´s poking his little dick into?"[23] This and the matter that she does not have any close relationships with friends or family shows that she finds herself stuck. Also the fact that she admits that she had an affair

---

[16] Albee: Three Tall Women (1994), p.30.
[17] Zinman: Edward Albee (2008), p.121.
[18] ibid.: p.121.
[19] Albee: Three Tall Women (1994), p.14.
[20] ibid.: p.14.
[21] ibid.: p.18.
[22] ibid.: p.10.
[23] ibid.: p.48.

and tells C: "What are you expecting? Monogamy or something?" [24], makes her appear a very resentful character.

A as the most important character, which already lived her whole life, is portrayed as a confused, imperious and charmless 92-year-old. She switches her mood between talking about stories of her life in a childish enthusiasm (see Albee, 1994, p.13), starting to cry because she forgot what she was going to say (see Albee, 1994, p.7) and being demanding towards B telling her what she has to do (see Albee, 1994, p.10). When B asks her if she is sitting cozily and admires a pillow, she responds: "(*Petulant*.) Of *course* I´m not comfortable; of *course* I want my pillow." [25] Simultaneously by not being able to take care of herself physically, she wants to be responsible for her own financial affairs. "(*Proud*.) [...] I wanted everything to be *right*; and I do now; I still do!" [26] is what she says but actually fails. On account of that C came to take care of her "unpaid bills". [27] When her husband died her wealth diminished. But because she wants to keep her high standard of living she sells some jewelry her husband gave her (see Albee, 1994, p.49). During the play it becomes clear that she found herself stuck in life when she was at B's age due to receiving more materialistic things than emotional affection from her husband (see Albee, 1994, p.28). But in the years following she gained peace with this question: "[...] *We* cheat for *lots* of reasons. Men cheat for only one – as you say, because they´re men." [28] That is why she does not see herself as a troubled woman. Instead she makes the people around her appear insufficient and inadequate. People who she "had to stay one step ahead of *all* of them [and; DD] fixed ´em [, her husband´s family; DD]." [29] She demonstrates friendship as an arrangement where she has to sacrifice time of her life and gets companionship in return (see Albee, 1994, p.22). But A remonstrates about her former acquaintances by saying: "You count on them! And they change. [...] They die; they go away. Nobody should *do* this!" [30] Even if there is so much mistrust in people she clarifies that by telling the audience that she remembers her past in a good way (see Albee, 1994, p.34) and finds her happiest moment in death because there is nothing to be done anymore. In addition to that she

---

[24] Albee: Three Tall Women (1994), p.39.
[25] ibid.: p.10 f.
[26] ibid.: p.18.
[27] ibid.: p.21.
[28] ibid.: p.40.
[29] ibid.: p.26.
[30] ibid.: p.22.

reduces her hate towards her son. She confesses that she never forgave him but admits: "(*very calm; sad smile.*) [...] [to B; DD:] You *do* want to see him again. *Wait* twenty years."[31] Although she went through a lot of perfidiousness in her life she "[...] provides the backstory of a life of privilege and self-indulgence [...]."[32]

What is important is the fact that B says: "Maybe you changed; they say you changed; I haven´t noticed."[33] Watching A, B and C act it becomes obvious that all of them behave in a completely different ways and therefore she did change indeed. A and B even enjoy winding C up (see Albee, 1994, p.11). Both of them elucidate this by declaring they are annoyed by her youth and naivety and want her to grow up (see Albee, 1994, p.10/34). Even though during the play A, B and C demonstrate dislike towards each other and blame each other's attitudes towards life (see Albee, 1994, p.51 f.) they join their hands (see Albee, 1994, p.55) at the end of the play, which symbolizes the peaceful end to A´s entire life and at the same time concludes the play.

3.1.2. The protagonist's life and the psychological consequences

The question is risen: 'where were the seeds of the protagonist´s development planted?' How did she evolve from a naive young lady into an old anti-social woman? Paul Baltes, a German psychologist, divides the life span´s developmental psychology in seven guiding principles. The first basic one testifies that new requests exist in an altered situation in life. These are responsible for triggering life processes, which concern different reactions at different stages of one's life (see Lang/Martin/Pinquart, 2012, p.23). During the play while the actors are talking about their one existence, Baltes' view on the various changes that take place in a human being's life from birth to death become obvious. As she goes through life the many diverse incidents, favorable and not so favorable circumstances shape her progress and emotional growth.

The protagonist spent her early years with her conservative family belonging to the working class. She grew up with her younger sister, who she envied for her brightness (see Albee, 1994, p.22). Their parents are both described as "strict but fair".[34] Her father was a carpenter and her mother looked after the children and made them "eat everything

---

[31] Albee: Three Tall Women (1994), p.44.
[32] Zinman: Edward Albee (2008), p.122.
[33] Albee: Three Tall Women (1994), p.43.
[34] ibid.: p.21.

she put before [them; DD], and wash the dishes"[35]; to sum up, A says that their mother "made [them; DD] be[come; DD] proper young ladies."[36] All of them went to church every Sunday without fail (see Albee, 1994, p.21). When the siblings got older they moved into a pleasant and cozy apartment. But her mother forced her daughters to write letters home twice a week. Each one of them had to write a separate letter, which the mother was going to correct with statements like "That´s not true", "Don´t abbreviate" or "Your sister said the same thing". When she had corrected the letters she sent them back to the girls (see Albee, 1994, p.23). Even if it would seem that from A´s position she was given a good education from her mother it is obvious she did not really enjoy her mother´s parenting. An important point in the play is when A points out what her mother always said to her, B reacts by remarking: "My God! I haven´t heard that in a long time. (*Imitates.*) 'Don´t you get fresh!'"[37] This suggests that she was pressurized and under permanent supervision of her mother. According to Sigmund Freud there were no open spaces, which are necessary to create an own personality in the genital phase (see Grünig, 2004, p.8). Ergo she was actually not taught how to be self-reliant in her early adulthood even if she was forced to do housework. Actually this just prepared her for becoming a wife. When the sisters moved to the city even her father came to put up his furniture in their flat for them, although it had furnishing before. They were over cared for and overprotected when they should rather have learned to care for themselves.

As a result she was never capable of being self-reliant. This explains why she was always on the lookout for the right man to marry. Actually her parents interfered with that as well: "Mother taught us what the right one [, husband; DD] would be."[38] The only job she had as a young lady was being a mannequin in a famous boutique. In that place she enjoyed being watched by several people, in particular by men even though they were engaged (see Albee, 1994, p.35). Living far away from her parents gave the protagonist the opportunity to go dancing in the city. Through the stories told during the play it becomes obvious that sexuality filled a very big part of the protagonist´s life against her mother´s advice: "Don´t give it [, virginity; DD] away like it was nothing."[39]

---

[35] Albee: <u>Three Tall Women</u> (1994), p.20 f.
[36] ibid.: p.21.
[37] ibid.: p.20.
[38] ibid.: p.34.
[39] ibid.: p.37.

She was 'deflowered' while she stayed out late. In the play sexual intercourses are told in a vivid way and there is an animated description of how she was 'deflowered' by a "beautiful"[40] young man. This is shown when they were dancing, "he pressed himself against her exactly against where he [, his member; DD] wanted to be".[41] Furthermore he made many erotic advances. When they pressed their bodies against each other on the dance floor and she felt that "his muscle was hard", she asked him what that meant, he repeated: "It´s me in love with you"[42]. He is described as a "good boy with coal-black hair and violet eyes and such a smile!"[43] They were the same height. Once the young man suggested that they go to his place because he did not want to be embarrassed right in front of the others, the protagonist heard herself saying: "I´m not that kind of girl"[44]. His reply was as follows: "yes you are, you're that kind of girl"[45] and they left. She notes the experience as a wonderful one, but adds that she was not really interested in him, because she was probably on a quest for a man worthy of her mother´s approval. One can say that her mother taught their daughters to find a wealthy man so as not to have to worry about money; that is what their parents possibly had to do. The fact that parents always want something better for their children is general knowledge. In consequence of the protagonist´s upbringing it is understandable that she comments in parts: "I´m a good girl, [and; DD] [...] I was a good girl."[46] What she says and how she behaves are two different things though. She was compelled to behave as a good girl. The remnant of her upbringing looms in her sexuality. Throughout her life she is incapable of performing oral sex even though she has tried and she tells B and C: "I just couldn´t: I can´t [conduct oral sex; DD]."[47] She tried because life is actually a discovery and not a compulsion from the exterior (see Freeman, 2013, p.227). In this specific case the protagonist´s mother forced her to behave in a proper way.

Her husband, who she married when she was 28 years old, is described as a little one-eyed man, who was rich and great company. Apparently he was the same man, who actually dated her sister (see Albee, 1994, p.39 ff.). Thereof her envy towards her sister becomes clear. She did not really care about this circumstance and made herself feel

---

[40] Albee: Three Tall Women (1994), p.36.
[41] ibid.: p.37.
[42] ibid.
[43] ibid.: p.36.
[44] ibid.: p.37.
[45] ibid.
[46] ibid.: p.38.
[47] ibid.

better because she achieved something her sister would not be capable of. Through that she got the recognition she was always searching for. Supplementary "costs and benefits [...] [are; DD] weigh[ed; DD] when making decisions."[48] She realized that in marrying him she would be taken care of financially and she did not mind doing it at her sister's expense. The protagonist had one child with her husband. Their son also comes on stage as the only wordless character in the play besides the three tall women. With her husband the protagonist moves into a big house with a separate stable for horses. As a couple they took an interest in horse-racing bets and overall they lead a comfortable life. At the age of 42 the protagonist has a horse-riding incident where she falls off the horse and breaks her back. She attributes the blame to the "stupid and cantankerous"[49] horse. That is proof for her lack of independence that is consistent through her life because she cannot accept fault since she never learned to assume responsibility. Additionally it can be recognized as a metaphor of the spinelessness she gained throughout the years.

After some time her mother moves into the house, where just the protagonist and her husband and their servants live. Since the passing away of her father - he died of heart failure when the protagonist turned 27 - the mother-daughter relationship rapidly deteriorated. When her son confides in her and tells her that he is homosexual their relationship experienced a total break-down. In the play it is manifested that he left home as a result of their clash. Twenty years later, the protagonist is about seventy, she wants to see him again because she has become lonely. The fact that her son returns home to see her after she had suffered a heart attack does not better the situation (see Albee, 1994, p.44). Even if he tries to be a good son superficially (see Albee, 1994, p.30), she never forgives him (see Albee, 1994, p.40). One can assume that she is not able of having a sane relationship with her own child because she never experienced one herself. Besides that, the protagonist is not capable of accepting her son's sexuality as a result of her upbringing. As already mentioned her parents had conservative views and consequently conveyed these opinions to their children. On the other hand she is in conflict with her mother because she pushed her in the way she did and gave her no space to forge her own opinions. "We all are positioned within our [...] socio-cultural, and social-psychological ways of living"[50], state Jack Martin and Alex Gillespie.

[48] Barresi/ Moore/ Raymond (2013), p.145.
[49] Albee: Three Tall Women (1994), p.48.
[50] Martin/ Gillespie (2013), p.163.

When she finds out about her husband's infidelity she as if to get even with him starts to cheat on him. She owns up to it: "I didn´t like sex much, but I had an affair."[51] Her only way to react is with revenge and that is what finally leads her to be unfaithful to her husband by having sex with their groom. Over the years and many incidents later their marriage became detached. The intimacy between her lover and her is also described in a very animated way by A.

The protagonist´s husband died when she was 66 because of prostate cancer. Afterwards she turns more and more into an insensitive person, who is not able to handle society any more. Around that time her mother dies. Because of their bad relationship, A says that she died as an enemy. Her sister became an alcoholic (see Albee, 1994, p.44). There is not much talk about her but it can be believed that the reasons of her emotional decay is her sister´s deception (see Albee, 1994, p.26) and that she could not handle life as she was brought up the same way as the protagonist. At the age of 92 A dies alone. Following Erik Erikson where integrity fights despair in old age, one can observe the achievement of integrity because the protagonist does not either commiserate or refuse her life (see Morse, 2005, p.33).

3.2. Analysis of the main themes connected to aging

In the following the three main themes will be analyzed because they have an important role in the psychology of aging. Just as appearance, memory and the attitude towards death change over the whole life-span of one person.

3.2.1. Appearances, vanity and beauty

For the protagonist her outer appearance and what people think about her is very important. The origin of that can be found in her upbringing. Conventions for her parents were relevant, as one can see that she was obliged to "wash everything [...] [she; DD] wore the night [...] [she; DD] wore it, by hand, before [...] [she; DD] went to bed."[52] In the play it becomes obvious that the protagonist cares very much about what to wear. For example when she went out dancing with her sister, they shared their clothes in a way so that the others, excessive fellows, would not notice they did (see Albee, 1994, p.23).

---

[51] Albee: Three Tall Women (1994), p.14 f.
[52] ibid.: p.21.

14

She was always concerned about her reputation. That is what she learned from her mother. "I'm a good girl"[53] is what she says but in contrast she behaves in a completely different way. For her it is more relevant to appear to be a well-behaved woman than actually being one. It is stated that when she went to school, she did not like being tall, even taller than the boys (see Albee, 1994, p.30). She did not want to protrude until she recognized that it was something special and even good to possess such a dainty height. Even her husband liked her because of that (see Albee, 1994, p.40). Coming from the working class, she was forced to adapt to the world of high society when she got married. Thereby she becomes conceited. In her early marriage when she went horse-riding one gets to know about her: "Never go out except you're properly dressed, I always said."[54] Living as a lady with a high social status makes her become vane. She cares about whether her jewelry is real or fake contrary to her 26-year-old version (see Albee, 1994, p.49 f.). Additionally she points out that she is 91 years old instead of the actual 92. C comments this with: "Vanity is amazing."[55] Her conceitedness makes her fight for even a year of difference in age. Actually her arm, that is heavily injured, should be amputated according to the doctor's advice, but she will not let him (see Albee, 1994, p.15 f.). She suffers from osteoporosis. She cannot cope with her body aging and instead she wants to remain tall, strong and young (see Albee, 1994, 24 f.). In the second act C reminds both of the others of their job as a mannequin. All of them walk around as if they were still in that shop. They become nostalgic together (see Albee, 1994, p.35).

3.2.2. Memory

Throughout the play one frequently encounters the word "remember". From the very beginning there is inconsistency between the protagonist's recollections of life - A, B and C connect several events with a completely different sentiment (see Albee, 1994, p.34). They have a complete individual thinking and feeling towards the same event and therefore could be strangers to one another even though they are the same person just at different stages of her life. The protagonist's attitude towards life changes with age. But something more interesting occurs in the play. According to Mark Freeman's studies of his demented mother there can be parallels seen between her and the woman in the

[53] Albee: Three Tall Women (1994), p.36.
[54] ibid.: p.5.
[55] ibid.: p.15.

drama. Sudden emotional outbursts, panic and desperate attempts are part of the symptoms (see Freeman, 2013, p.236). Thus it is not surprising that A breaks a glass for B´s displeasure and is delighted with her discrete action, then after a short shock stops and weeps until she is really startled and wants to know what everybody was talking about and then against all expectations is happy to spot C until she denies her own assertions (see Albee, 1994, p.16 f.). From time to time there are very specific memories, like when she is talking about her husband´s encounters (see Albee, 1994, p.28) and sometimes she does not know anything at all (see Albee, 1994, p.27). Further evidence for dementia is her use of words. The lasting loss of mental skills (see Knoll, 1979, p.59) is seen in her language. Even if she talks quite freely about sex, she calls the male member "pee-pee"[56]. When she sustains a short seizure she falls into a talking of confusion that prompts her to say that she cannot remember whether or not she loves her son (see Albee, 1994, p.30 f.).

3.2.3. Mortality and death

"In Act I, the three women embody three reactions to the process of aging that leads to death. The "smell of mortality" that hangs over the act is at first rejected, then defied, until at last listened to." [57]

Several times mortality is stated throughout the play. It is made sure and pointed out several times in the play that everybody is aware of death, but does not think of one´s own. For instance A says that she is perhaps the only one who does not perish while she is actually on her deathbed yet (see Albee, 1994, p.41). As already mentioned B is the one who talks more frequently about death. Her way of seeing life is that from the moment you are born you are already dying (see Albee, 1994, p.9). She sees demise in any condition whatsoever: "It's downhill from sixteen on! For all of us [sic!]!"[58] Because of her middle-age she becomes more aware of aging and what is lying ahead. Therefore it becomes obvious that C as the youngest version does not think of death at all in comparison to B. A - as the oldest one - does not fear death. Instead she is looking forward to it (see Albee, 1994, p.32) because she regards it as salvation. She looks back and is sure of a good past behind her and sees her life as fulfilled. Over and above the fact is proven that she overcame despair and gained integrity (see Morse, 2005, p.33).

---

[56] Albee: Three Tall Women (1994), p.29.
[57] Morse (2005), p.31.
[58] Albee: Three Tall Women (1994), p.9.

One shall be remembered of the last scene, where A puts out her hands to take B's and C's.

4. Conclusion: Children's upbringing as a matter of importance

"Why does a person become the way they are?" - This question arose while writing this paper. What stuck out was the most important factor that leads somebody to become the person standing in front of us in the end. It is the upbringing, the early experience we have in childhood. How one learns things and perceives its surrounding world. The origin of everybody's personality lies in the effects of the parents' upbringing. Hence accrues and develops the later attitude towards life. It is important for a child to be taught that there is more than only one view towards a circumstance. Open minds are necessary for building an individual opinion. Children shall experience issues in an objective way to be capable of learning and experiencing different ways of thinking. For instance the protagonist in <u>Three Tall Women</u>: if she had been capable of changing her role from the "good girl" that she was pushed into, she would have become more self-sufficient and at peace with herself and perhaps her life would have taken an absolutely different course. Because upbringing can affect how a person lives their whole life. Sigmund Freud's advice for bringing up children is an extraordinary achievement. Nurture can be compared to societal systems but in a minor dimension. A division, hierarchical class structures or inequitable privilege can exist. Maybe one is not capable of changing these systems but in case of the upbringing it is necessary to choose an open-minded, equal and pleasurable setting for one's children own good.

5. Bibliography

5.1. Primary literature

Albee, Edward: Three Tall Women. New York, Dramatists Play Service, 1994.

5.2. Secondary literature

Barresi, John / Moore, Chris / Martin, Raymond: "Conceiving of self and others as persons: evolution and development". In: Jack Martin/ Mark H. Bickhard: The psychology of personhood. Philosophical, Historical, Social- Developmental and Narrative Perspectives. Cambridge University Press, New York, 2013.

Freeman, Mark: "Storied persons, The double triad of narrative identity". In: Jack Martin/ Mark H. Bickhard: The psychology of personhood. Philosophical, Historical, Social- Developmental and Narrative Perspectives. Cambridge University Press, New York, 2013.

Frieder R. Lang/Mike Martin/Martin Pinquart: Entwicklungspsychologie – Erwachsenenalter. Göttingen, Hogrefe Verlag, 2012.

Grünig, Sabine: Die Grundlagen der Psychoanalyse nach Sigmund Freud. Grin, Frankfurt am Main, 2004

Knoll, Ludwig: Lexikon der praktischen Psychologie: Erkenntnisse und Argumente zur Menschenkunde im Alltag. Bergisch Gladbach, Lübbe, 1979.

Martin, Jack/ Gillespie, Alex: "Position exchange theory and personhood: moving between positions and perspectives within physical, socio- cultural and psychological space and time". In: Jack Martin/ Mark H. Bickhard: The psychology of personhood. Philosophical, Historical, Social- Developmental and Narrative Perspectives. Cambridge University Press, New York, 2013.

Morse, Donald E.: "Present at the End: Performing Mortality in King Lear and Three Tall Women". In: Michael Keneally/Rhona Richman Keneally (Ed.): From 'English Literature' to 'Literatures in English'. International Perspectives. Festschrift in Honour of WOLFGANG ZACH. Winter, Heidelberg, 2005. P. 27-36

Zinman, Toby: Edward Albee. Ann Arbor, 2008.

5.3.Online resources

Academy of Achievement, a museum of living history (2008): Edward Albee: Edward Albee Interview. http://www.achievement.org/autodoc/page/alb1int-1, retrieved 25.05.2013

Academy of Achievement, a museum of living history (2010): Edward Albee: Edward Albee Biography. http://www.achievement.org/autodoc/page/alb1bio-1, retrieved 20.05.2013

Charles Newell (2011): Edward Albee's Three Tall. http://www.courttheatre.org/season/show/three_tall_women/, retrieved 21.05.2013

National Public Radio (2011): Playwright Edward Albee defends 'Gay Writer' Remarks. http://www.npr.org/2011/06/06/136923478/playwright-edward-albee-defends-remarks, retrieved 25.05.2013